Victoria Falls

'Avatar' Mountain

Northern Lights

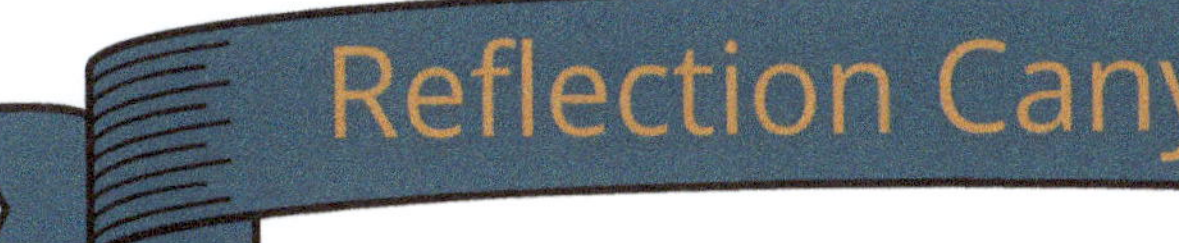

Reflection Canyon

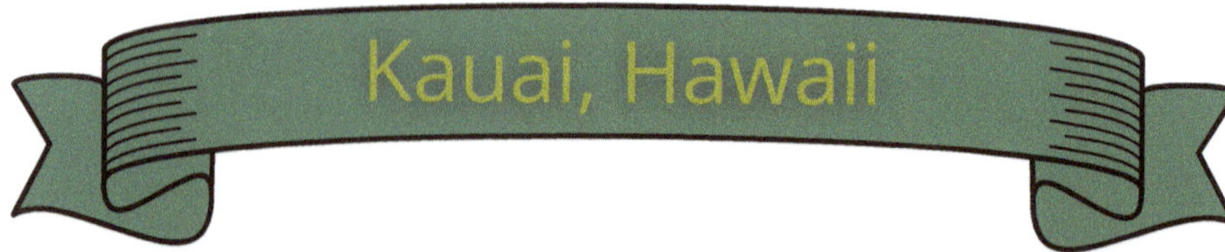
Kauai, Hawaii

Ko Phi Phi

Louise & Moraine

Half Dome, Yosemite

Mount Everest

Galapagos Islands

Socotra

Deadvlei & Namib-Naukluft

Yellowstone

Salkantay Inca Trek

El Nido, Palavan

Arches National Park

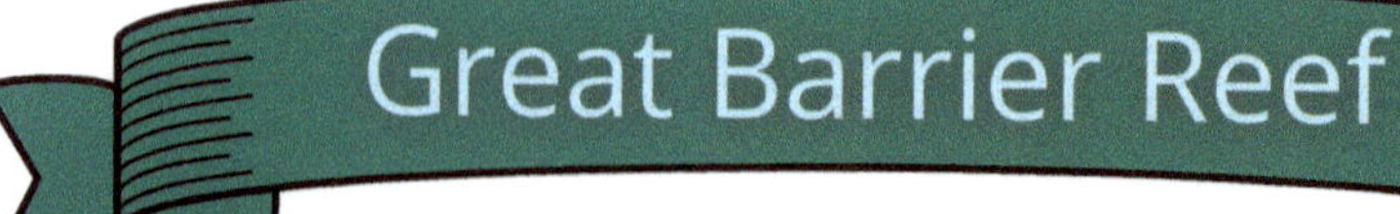

Great Barrier Reef

Lakes of Mt. Kelimutu

Grand Canyon

Salar de Uyuni

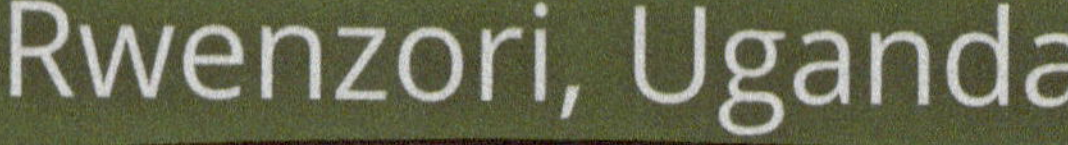

Rwenzori, Uganda

Lake O'hara

Zion National Park

Grand Teton

Wadi Rum, Jordan

Trang An and Tam Coc

Dades Gorge

Vinales Valley

Antelope Canyon

Taroko National Park

Crater Lake

Jasper National Park

Ha Long Bay

Okavango delta

Bisti Wilderness

Nyiragongo Volcano

Gros Morne National Park

Garibaldi Provincial

Stone forest

Pamukkale, Turkey

Colca Canyon

Garden of The Gods

Hunza Valley

Hoh Rainforest

Mt. Robson

Phang NGA Bay

Rocky Mountain

Black Canyon

Tiger Leaping Gorge

Coyote Gulch

Drakensberg

White Sands, New Mexico

North Cascades

Chiricahua

Huascaran National Park

Mount Kenya

Tianmen Mountain

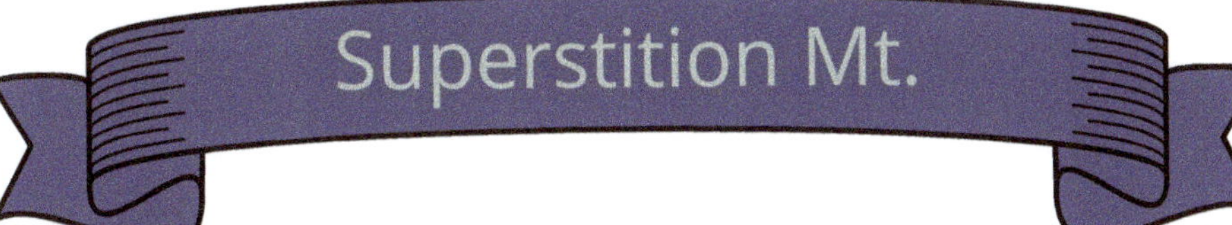
Superstition Mt.

Mount Rinjani

Quebrada de las